INFORMATION
TECHNOLOGY

STEVE SLEIGHT

DK

A Dorling Kindersley Book

Dorling DK Kindersley

LONDON, NEW YORK, SYDNEY, DELHI, PARIS
MUNICH & JOHANNESBURG

Senior Editor Adèle Hayward
Senior Designer Caroline Marklew
DTP Designer Jason Little
Production Controllers Elizabeth
Cherry, Heather Hughes

Senior Managing Editor Stephanie
Jackson
Managing Art Editor Nigel Duffield
US Editor Gary Werner

Produced for Dorling Kindersley by

studio **cactus** ●

13 SOUTHGATE STREET WINCHESTER HAMPSHIRE SO23 9DZ

Editor Sue Gordon
Designer Laura Watson

First published in the United States by
Dorling Kindersley Publishing, Inc.
95 Madison Avenue
New York, New York 10016

First American Edition, 2000

2 4 6 8 10 9 7 5 3 1

CIP data available on request
ISBN 0-7894-5970-1

Reproduced by Colourscan, Singapore
Printed in Hong Kong by Wing King Tong Co. Ltd.

See our complete catalogue at
www.dk.com

CONTENTS

INTRODUCTION

Nowadays, information technology permeates virtually every aspect of modern business, to the extent that its effective use can easily mean the difference between success and failure. Managers in every field, from human resources to marketing, must understand the implications and quickly learn how to benefit from the new industrial revolution. Information Technology will help you to break through the jargon and mystique that often surrounds the subject and face up to the challenge of IT. Practical advice helps you to deal with the business issues, gives you the confidence to use and manage IT, and shows you how you to profit from the Internet revolution. There is further assistance in the form of 101 concise tips, and a self-assessment exercise allows you to evaluate your IT skills.

FACING THE CHALLENGE OF IT

To be successful in today's fast-changing, highly competitive business world, it is vital that an organization uses IT effectively. Ensure that you and your staff fully accept the need to learn.

UNDERSTANDING IT

The effective use of IT is one of the biggest challenges facing most organizations today. Understanding the role IT plays and how to make the best use of IT systems is an essential requirement for any organization seeking competitive advantage.

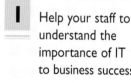

1 Help your staff to understand the importance of IT to business success.

CULTURAL DIFFERENCES

American military, research, and commercial organizations led the development of information technology, but today its use has spread worldwide. The US still leads in the production of IT tools, but European countries, India, and others are carving out their own technology niches.

WHAT IS IT?

IT stands for information technology and, in its widest sense, refers to any technology controlled by a microprocessor (or computer chip). For example, microprocessors are used to control the delivery of essential services such as water, electricity, and telecommunications. They are also a crucial part of most types of manufacturing and distribution processes. However, most managers' involvement with IT is limited to two types of computer systems: those that store and manipulate data, and those that provide fast and efficient communication between people and businesses.

2 Look for new technologies that make work easier.

3 Focus on how IT can empower you and your business.

BENEFITING FROM IT

There is no organization that can afford to ignore the empowering technology of the modern world. Today's IT systems can help a business to be more responsive, efficient, and flexible in the face of continuous and rapid change. Properly used, information technology will allow your company to streamline its processes and focus on the core skills and abilities that differentiate it from its competitors in the marketplace. Failure to embrace the opportunities that are offered by IT today is likely to result in business failure.

MAKING THE MOST OF IT

Using the power of modern IT systems to best advantage is a strategic skill that has become an essential requirement if an organization is to keep ahead of its competitors. IT fulfills many functions in an organization, including automated process and systems; but for managers the key role is as an enabling technology. Managers must select and use IT systems to communicate more efficiently, to simplify business processes, and to acquire, analyze, and manage the data on which their business depends.

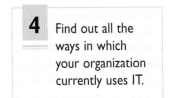

4 Find out all the ways in which your organization currently uses IT.

▼ **USING IT EFFECTIVELY**
Making effective use of the power of IT offers important benefits at both a personal and an organizational level.

PERSONAL ASPECTS | BUSINESS ASPECTS

IT can help me work smarter, not harder

IT allows me to work away from the office

IT keeps me informed, even on the move

IT can get me closer to my customers

IT can help me to reduce costs

IT can make my business more flexible

HARNESSING THE POWER OF IT

To gain maximum benefit from the use of IT, an organization must ensure that systems are truly effective in meeting its needs. Decision-makers must create efficient ownership of technology, and should focus on using IT to gain competitive advantage.

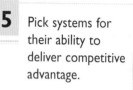

5 Pick systems for their ability to deliver competitive advantage.

CREATING EFFECTIVE SYSTEMS

IT is a business tool that can radically improve the way you manage your business and communicate with your key audiences. If systems are to deliver real benefits, they must be:

- Transparent to the user: users do not need to know how systems work; the requirement is simply that they perform as and when needed.
- Fast and easy to use: users should find systems simple to use, and must be able to complete tasks quickly without having to wait any significant time for the system to respond.
- Flexible: changing needs require systems that are capable of being adapted quickly.

DEPENDING ON IT ▲
Many organizations—for example, financial markets—rely totally on efficient IT systems in order to conduct business.

HIGHLIGHTING NEEDS

Organizations need to be responsive to changing markets; they must act quickly to develop new products and satisfy customer expectations. To help create competitive advantage, IT systems must be focused on real business needs. Give departmental users the power to identify their specific needs and then request IT solutions, rather than allowing an IT department to impose technology-led systems.

6 Design technology to fit the business needs, not the other way around.

DECIDING WHO MANAGES THE IT RESOURCE

An important consideration when selecting new systems or changing to new technologies is who will manage the resource. All systems must be maintained and monitored so that failures and downtime are kept to an absolute minimum. If a new technology is being introduced, make sure that your IT staff understand it fully and are capable of managing it. If in any doubt, arrange for IT staff to have training, or contract with the supplier for external support services.

TAKING OWNERSHIP

Given that the effective use of IT is a strategically important corporate skill, the issue of who controls IT is absolutely critical. In the past, the IT function often reported to a chief financial officer, who may not have fully understood the technology. Today, it is vital to have an IT-literate person on the board, as well as in each department, of your organization. The senior person focuses the use of IT on the organization's current and future needs, while the departmental champions promote its efficient use.

7 For speed and flexibility, keep IT systems simple.

8 Learn about IT and promote its use in your team.

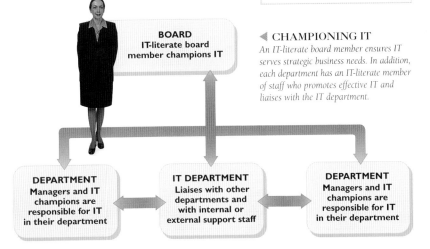

BOARD
IT-literate board member champions IT

◀ CHAMPIONING IT
An IT-literate board member ensures IT serves strategic business needs. In addition, each department has an IT-literate member of staff who promotes effective IT and liaises with the IT department.

DEPARTMENT
Managers and IT champions are responsible for IT in their department

IT DEPARTMENT
Liaises with other departments and with internal or external support staff

DEPARTMENT
Managers and IT champions are responsible for IT in their department

FOCUSING ON THE HUMAN ELEMENT

While great effort is put into developing better, faster, and more complex IT systems, the human element is often ignored. If the full value of IT is to be realized, you must ensure that users feel in control of the technology and are positive about its use.

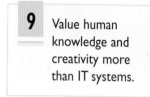

9 Value human knowledge and creativity more than IT systems.

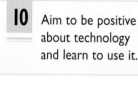

10 Aim to be positive about technology and learn to use it.

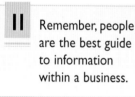

11 Remember, people are the best guide to information within a business.

TAKING CONTROL

It is very common for people to fear technology when they do not feel in control of it. This is especially true when the technology is obviously complicated and involves the use of jargon that alienates the uninitiated. In contrast to other complex technologies, such as television or the telephone system, IT systems are still prone to failures and are not yet transparent to users. The user must learn a new language and significant new skills to get the best from IT. You and your staff will feel in control only when you make an effort to learn about the technology.

BEING POSITIVE

It is important for your career as a manager that you understand the business implications of IT and learn how to use common systems. Start by eliminating negative attitudes to technology and focus on its benefits. After all, this technology is not going away; indeed, it will increasingly have impact on every aspect of your life. Make a decision to learn how to use IT and seek out colleagues who can help you. Jargon is often a barrier to learning, so ask them to avoid its use, or explain key terms.

QUESTIONS TO ASK YOURSELF

Q Have I made sufficient effort to learn about technology and the IT systems I use at work?

Q Am I being positive enough about the use and value of IT in my organization?

Q Do I understand the technology enough to feel in control of the systems I use?

HOW PEOPLE ADD ▼ VALUE TO INFORMATION

Data becomes information only when it is interpreted and put in context by an analyst. A decision-maker uses information to plan actions and inform staff.

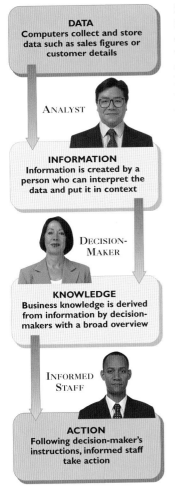

DATA
Computers collect and store data such as sales figures or customer details

ANALYST

INFORMATION
Information is created by a person who can interpret the data and put it in context

DECISION-MAKER

KNOWLEDGE
Business knowledge is derived from information by decision-makers with a broad overview

INFORMED STAFF

ACTION
Following decision-maker's instructions, informed staff take action

CREATING AN INFORMATION CULTURE

The lifeblood of any organization is information, and IT systems are often created to manage, store, and distribute it. However, many of these systems fail to achieve their objectives. A common reason for this is the tendency to focus on technological capabilities rather than how people actually work with information. This usually creates a rigid, computer-centered view, rather than a flexible, human-centered, and often disordered one, which reflects the way people actually use and share information. Equally common is the assumption that people will naturally share information if they have the technology to do so. In fact, when information means power, people are unlikely to share key information unless the culture of the company encourages them to do so. So it is important to create an information culture before using IT to assist in its management.

12 Ensure people learn good inter-personal skills before relying on IT-based communication tools.

DO'S AND DON'TS

✔ Do be prepared to acknowledge that you don't understand your colleagues' IT jargon.

✔ Do consider how people naturally use and share information.

✔ Do create incentives to encourage the sharing of information.

✘ Don't use jargon when explaining IT to new computer users.

✘ Don't expect people to share valuable information if the culture is competitive.

✘ Don't try to use IT to solve problems that are people-based.

KEEPING UP WITH CHANGE

A common complaint concerns the difficulty of keeping up with changes in IT systems, which seem to be developing at breakneck speed. Managers must learn to recognize and respond to IT developments that are relevant to their organization.

13 Accept that change is inevitable and look for ways to use it to advantage.

THINGS TO DO

1. Focus on technologies that offer demonstrable benefit.
2. Be prepared to allocate time to stay in touch with new developments.
3. Develop contacts with colleagues who are better than you in the use of IT tools.
4. Explain your key needs to the IT department.

ACCEPTING CHANGE

Change in the business environment is caused by technological developments and the increasing globalization of markets, but it is in the use of IT that the speed of change is most apparent. Even IT experts complain that it is difficult to keep up to date with changes in technology, so it is perfectly understandable that most managers feel that keeping up is beyond their skills, or that they do not have time. However, it is extremely important to be aware of changes that may iinfluence your business or job. The pace of change will not slow down in the near future, and those unwilling or unable to adapt quickly could find themselves out of business while more flexible competitors succeed.

BEING SELECTIVE

Don't try to keep up with all changes. Instead, be selective and concentrate on learning about new tools or technologies that can make important tasks easier, save you time, or help cut business costs or increase profits. Look for IT systems that are of strategic or operational importance to your business. Increasingly, these will include Internet e-commerce systems (for buying and selling on the Internet), or an intranet (a private website) for internal information management. Identify the key areas and concentrate on their development.

14 Harness useful changes faster than your competitors.

15 Help your team focus on changes that are significant.

MONITORING NEW DEVELOPMENTS

The only way to stay in touch with fast-changing technology is to allocate a small amount of time, on a regular basis, to monitor the developments in those areas that are important to you. The best sources of information are the Internet, specialized magazines, reports on technology in general media, and colleagues who are IT-literate and use similar technology. If your organization has an IT department, ask it to keep you informed of important changes. Show interest in, and ask questions about, technology that is important to you. If you use commercial software, visit the maker's website regularly to get details of bugs, upgrades, and usage tips. Many software suppliers publish Internet mailing lists through which you can receive regular product information.

16 Use the Internet as your main research tool.

QUESTIONS TO ASK YOURSELF

Q Are the hardware or software tools I use up to date or have they been superseded?

Q Are there features in other tools that would make me or my business more efficient?

Q Has the latest software been fully tested by others so that I can be sure there are no major problems?

One team member is responsible for reading specialized magazines

IT champion updates team on relevant developments

Departmental manager keeps focus on business issues and needs

KEEPING UP WITH ▲ NEW DEVELOPMENTS
Hold regular meetings with your staff to share information on new hardware or software that might have implications for your organization's performance.

17 Keep an eye on Internet-led changes, since these will have the most impact on your business.

LOOKING AT IT ON THE DESKTOP

A wide perspective on IT is essential if managers are to pick solutions that match the needs of their organization and staff. Gain a full understanding of common hardware and software tools.

FINDING THE RIGHT TOOLS

Selecting the most appropriate technology and systems for your particular needs is a vital first step in making the best use of IT. These decisions can have long-term implications, so you should involve system-users and IT staff in the selection process.

18 Learn about the technologies that are leading current IT developments.

POINTS TO REMEMBER

● IT systems have gone through many developments. Many of the old systems are still in use and must be allowed for when adding new systems or technologies.

● Sharing data between old systems and modern, Internet-based ones can be difficult, time-consuming, and expensive.

● Doing business electronically requires IT systems that are compatible (or work) with the standards used on the Internet.

CHOOSING APPROPRIATE TECHNOLOGY

IT systems have changed considerably in just a few years, with the result that many organizations have a mixture of old (legacy) systems and newer technology. Today's IT systems are being driven by Internet technology as most organizations rush to exploit the medium and to run intranets (private websites) on their internal networks. If you need to select new systems, look for ones that will work with "open" (published) Internet standards to give maximum flexibility. They must also be able to communicate with any legacy systems you have.

EXPLAINING BASIC JARGON

KEY TERM	DEFINITION
Bit	The smallest unit of information that a computer can process.
Byte	One character (a number, letter, or symbol). Made up of eight bits.
CD-ROM	Removable compact disc (CD) for read-only memory (ROM).
Chip	The computer's microprocessor, which controls its functions.
DVD	Removable digital versatile disc (DVD), which is superseding CDs.
Hard disc	The computer's permanent data storage device. Also called the hard drive.
Hardware	The physical, visible components of a computer system.
Operating System	Software that controls a computer's overall operation.
RAM	Random Access Memory: impermanent working storage within a computer.
Software	Electronic instructions for the computer, which run on hardware.

ASSESSING TOOLS

The starting point for assessing new IT tools must always be the business requirement, not any aspect of technology. First, clearly define the tasks that the tools must perform, then examine the potential solutions that are available. Benchmark your competitors, if possible, to find the systems they have chosen, and draw up a shortlist for further consideration. Do not rely on technical specifications or the promises of sales people.

19 Ask for a trial when considering new IT tools.

▼ CHOOSING CAREFULLY
Take time to make a considered judgment when selecting a new system. It may have to last for some years. Involve users and focus on business benefits.

Assess likely future business needs	→	Involve users in the selection process	→	Carry out trials on shortlisted systems

IDENTIFYING THE COMPONENTS

It is not necessary to understand how a computer works to make effective use of it, but you will achieve better results when working with IT systems if you have a good understanding of the roles of the various hardware devices and software programs.

20 Add more RAM to speed performance when using large programs or files.

UNDERSTANDING YOUR COMPUTER

The chips and circuitry that are the heart of a computer reside in the computer case. Input and output devices (known as peripherals) are connected to this by cables or infrared devices. When the computer is working with data, it stores it in its active, primary storage—called Random Access Memory (RAM). Adding more RAM is an effective, easy way to boost your computer's performance. A magnetic hard disc in the computer case provides permanent storage. Modern hard discs store several gigabytes (GB) of data. Extra storage is provided by removable media such as CD-Roms.

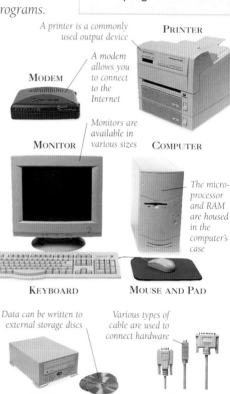

A printer is a commonly used output device

PRINTER

A modem allows you to connect to the Internet

MODEM

Monitors are available in various sizes

MONITOR

COMPUTER

The microprocessor and RAM are housed in the computer's case

KEYBOARD

MOUSE AND PAD

Data can be written to external storage discs

Various types of cable are used to connect hardware

CD BURNER

CABLES

HARDWARE COMPONENTS ▶
Many types of input and output devices can be connected to allow you to input data and retrieve it in a usable form.

UNDERSTANDING HARDWARE

The term hardware refers to all the physical parts of your computer, the network it is connected to, and any peripherals (attached devices). Although computer hardware is often technologically outdated within a year or so of purchase, most organizations find it can handle the tasks required of it for up to a decade. Equally, since standard business software rarely requires the speed and power of the latest computers on the market, you will find it is not normally necessary to buy the fastest computers available.

QUESTIONS TO ASK YOURSELF

Q How old is my computer hardware, and is it obsolete?

Q Am I kept waiting while my computer performs processing tasks?

Q Can I add more RAM to speed up my computer?

Q Does my software perform all the tasks I need?

Q Do I need new hardware to run the software I need?

 21 Choose leading suppliers for your equipment needs.

 22 Have at least 32MB of RAM to suit the memory needs of modern programs.

UNDERSTANDING SOFTWARE

The term software refers to the invisible parts of a computer system that provide the functionality and flexibility to perform useful work. System software, usually called the operating system (OS), controls the computer (and all communication with attached devices), provides the user interface (what is visible on screen), and acts as an intermediary for application software. Applications are software programs designed for specific tasks, such as accounting or word processing. A huge number of applications exist to cater for virtually any need.

ESTABLISHING PRIORITIES

Ideally, you should first select the application software best suited to the particular needs of your organization, and then choose hardware and an operating system that meet the requirements of those software packages. However, unless you are installing computer hardware for the first time, or are ready to upgrade existing equipment, you will have to pick from applications that will run on the hardware you have installed.

23 Remember that you do not need the latest, powerful computer chips to run most business software.

17

SELECTING HARDWARE

Choosing hardware can seem confusing because of the complicated technical specifications that are often quoted. In fact, it is not difficult, even for nontechnical managers, to select suitable computers, monitors, and basic input devices.

24 Remember that "Wintel" PCs and Macs can share the same network.

25 Ensure that you take maintenance costs into account.

POINTS TO REMEMBER

- Stability and reliability are most important for business use.

- Powerful computers are needed for multimedia applications such as website design, graphic design, and video or audio editing.

- Less power is needed for most business desktop computers than home ones designed for games and multimedia applications.

- Modern, "multisync" monitors allow you to adjust screen resolution according to the need.

CHOOSING COMPUTERS

In many business situations the decisions about computer selection and purchase are made by IT staff, but in smaller organizations the task may fall to nontechnical managers. Most modern personal computers will be fast enough for common business applications, so you should focus on issues such as ease of use, ownership cost (on-going costs, including dealing with problems and breakdowns), and reliability. The standard business desktop PC has an Intel processor and one of the Windows operating systems (often called a Wintel machine), but Apple Macintosh computers (Macs) are a worthy alternative, as are PCs running the Linux OS. Macs have a strong reputation as fast and user-friendly, with a low total cost of ownership, and are often chosen for creative and multimedia work.

Check that the supplier can provide the aftersales service you require.

Make a list of the features you need, and compare potential products against your checklist

MAKING THE DECISION ▶
Use a checklist to assess the merits of possible products, then discuss your specific requirements with the suppliers.

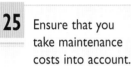

Monitor should display at least 256 colors

Picture is made up of vertical and horizontal dots, called pixels (picture elements)

Resolution describes number of pixels per inch, horizontally and vertically. A low-resolution monitor may display 640x480 pixels, a high-resolution 1280x1024 pixels

Thousands, or millions, of colors are used for design work

DECIDING ON A MONITOR

A standard monitor has a CRT (cathode-ray tube), like a TV set. Size is measured diagonally across the picture tube but the visible area is slightly smaller. A 15-inch screen is standard for most business applications, but a 17- or 21-inch screen is better for large spreadsheets or graphics work. LCD (liquid crystal display) screens are used on laptops, and may well become the norm for desktop use.

▲ **CHOOSING RESOLUTION**
A high resolution shows more information on screen because the images are smaller than on a low-resolution display.

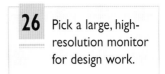

26 Pick a large, high-resolution monitor for design work.

Most keyboards have a standard layout

Mouse pad used under mouse

Drawing tablet and pen useful for precise graphic or technical work

INPUTTING TOOLS ▲
Various designs of keyboards, mice, and drawing tablets are available. Choose ones that are well made and comfortable to use for long periods.

CHOOSING A KEYBOARD AND MOUSE

The keyboard and mouse are the primary means of entering information and controlling the computer. Keyboards vary in quality and feel, so try out different makes before making your choice. Some have a shaped wrist support that can increase comfort when typing, and help reduce wrist and finger strain. The mouse is used to control a pointer that selects and moves objects on the screen. It is usually connected to the keyboard by a thin cable, but cordless types are available. Mice are made in different shapes and sizes, and have one, two, or three buttons.

PUTTING INFORMATION IN

Input devices are used to communicate with the computer and to transfer information into it so that the data can be processed. The keyboard is the most commonly used input device, but there are many others available to suit the type of data you need to capture. For instance, a bar-code reader transfers data from a printed bar code into a stock system, and a voice input system allows you to use speech to control the computer.

27 For fast scanning of small amounts of data, use a handheld scanner.

COMMON INPUT DEVICES

HARDWARE	WHAT IS IT? HOW IS IT USED?
BAR-CODE READER	A bar-code reader is needed to scan the black-and-white bars that are used to store product details, and to transfer the data into a computer. Typical uses are point-of-sale applications, distribution control, and the tracking of supplies and products.
DIGITAL CAMERA	The latest digital stills and video cameras are very effective and can be plugged directly into a computer. This makes it possible to edit the images on-screen and quickly incorporate them into a brochure, catalogue, or presentation.
MICROPHONE	Modern desktop computers now allow the use of speech recognition to control the computer. In addition, text can be dictated directly into a word-processing program. This is extremely useful, especially for inexperienced typists.
NETWORK CONNECTION	A network connection gives access to information stored on other computers or storage devices on the network. If the network is also connected to the Internet, users can access and input information from innumerable sources worldwide.
SCANNER	A scanner is a useful office tool used to capture an image of a document or graphic that can then be manipulated and stored in the computer. An optical character recognition program (OCR) is used to convert scanned text into an editable form.

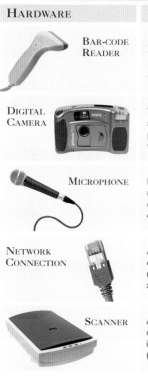

GETTING INFORMATION OUT

Output devices are used to convert digital computer information into other forms, or to transfer information to other equipment or storage media. A monitor is an output device that allows you to view and interact with text and images displayed on its screen. Other devices include printers, plotters for large graphics or technical drawings, and audio speakers. Connection to a network allows data to be shared with others.

28 Remember, a Zip disc has much more capacity than the old floppy disc.

COMMON OUTPUT DEVICES

HARDWARE	WHAT IS IT? HOW IS IT USED?
STORAGE MEDIA	Removable storage media range from floppy discs storing 1.4MB (megabytes) to CD-ROM and DVD discs with capacities of 650MB or up to 9GB (gigabytes). These allow easy storage or distribution of video or multimedia information.
FAX MODEM	Faxing a document directly from your computer is far more efficient than printing it out and sending it from a fax machine. This is achieved simply by connecting your computer to a fax modem, either directly or via a network.
INKJET PRINTER	Inkjet printers are not as fast as laser printers and their print quality is slightly lower, but they can produce good results in full color at a much lower cost than a laser printer. They are ideal for users who require low-cost, color-printed output.
LASER PRINTER	A laser printer is the standard choice for an office because it provides high-speed printing with high-quality output. A laser printer can be connected directly to the user's computer or, more commonly, to a network so that it can be shared.
VIDEO TAPE	Both audio and video can be edited on computer and then output to a variety of media including tape, CD-ROM, and DVD discs. Audio/video presentations can be run from the computer using speakers and projection equipment.

USING NETWORKS

*N*etworks are the arteries of modern business and are vital for sharing information and communication both inside and outside the organization. A network system must be selected to suit the number of users and to provide fast file-sharing.

29 Select a network that will run quickly, even when sharing large files.

30 Use a laptop for working on the move, and connect to the office network to share files.

SHARING INFORMATION

Information stored on a computer that is not connected to a network can be shared only by printing it out or by copying it to a removable disk. A network solves this problem, and allows a group of computers to share files and have access to other devices, such as printers and scanners, that are also connected to the network. Networks must transfer files at sufficient speed to prevent delays in working. When all the computers are in the same department or building, the network is called a Local Area Network (LAN).

KEEPING THINGS SIMPLE

The simplest form of network is a peer-to-peer arrangement, which provides a low-cost way of connecting a small number of computers (usually fewer than 10) in the same office. Each user's files are stored on his or her own computer, but anyone on the network can be given access to those files. Because the files are all stored on individual computers, they can be difficult to manage efficiently, but a peer-to-peer network does mean that if one computer fails, the others on the network are still usable. Since any standard desktop system can manage file-transfer tasks, a peer-to-peer network does not require a more powerful, special network-operating system.

THINGS TO DO

1. Decide on the number of users who need to be connected to the network.

2. Consider the size of files that you need to transfer: large multimedia files need higher network capacity than text files.

3. Decide whether a peer-to-peer or client/server network is more appropriate for your needs.

INTERNET CONNECTION

PRINTER

CLIENT

CLIENT

CLIENT

SERVER

A COMMON ▲ CLIENT/SERVER NETWORK

A client/server network links all users with a powerful central server and with input or output devices connected to the network.

31 Consider installing two servers to avoid network loss if one fails.

32 Use passwords to control user access to the server, its files, and folders.

SERVICING THE LARGER ORGANIZATION

An organization that has more than about 10 computers requires a more sophisticated network if it is to share information effectively. The most common type is called a client/server system, in which users' computers (clients) are connected to a central, more powerful computer called a server. All data files are stored on the server, which usually has extra-large hard discs and a powerful server-operating system. Because all the files are stored centrally, they can be organized easily, protected against viruses, and backed up regularly (by being saved to another storage device) to prevent loss of valuable data. The server also controls communications, managing the performance of the network and controlling users' access to the Internet or to fax facilities. If the server fails, however, all users will be affected.

23

HARNESSING INTERNET STANDARDS

Early networks used several different, and often incompatible, systems to transfer information; but the growth of the Internet has transformed network systems. By using software and hardware tools that conform to Internet standards, you achieve compatibility with the Internet and the ability to build an intranet (a private, internal website). This gives you an efficient, low-cost method of sharing your information internally and across the Internet.

33 Use network systems compatible with the Internet.

34 Create an intranet for easy sharing of information.

35 Plan a network to cope with the demands of users for fast, reliable data sharing.

MOVING OUTSIDE YOUR NETWORK

The usefulness of a network can be extended considerably, especially if it is based on Internet standards. A LAN can be connected to other LANs within the organization, even in other cities or countries, by creating a Wide Area Network (WAN) using dedicated telephone lines. Or you can ask your Internet Service Provider (ISP) to set up a Virtual Private Network (VPN), on which information is encrypted for privacy before being sent across the Internet. An Internet connection also provides you with access to global email, the Web, and other resources.

◀ SETTING UP A SIMPLE NETWORK

This case study shows that setting up a simple network need not be complicated or require a lot of technical knowledge. The job can be done quickly and cost-effectively, yet it can also deliver real benefits to staff, the organization, and clients.

CASE STUDY

Fiona, director of a small PR agency, was asked to organize the networking of computers in a regional office. The office had eight unconnected computers, requiring staff to use floppy discs to exchange files. Staff were now asking for the ability to share files and to have email. Fiona started by employing a consultant to advise on networking issues and decided to include the requirement to give staff access to the Internet, initially for email only. Together with the consultant, Fiona reviewed the performance of the existing computers and decided to upgrade the four oldest. A simple peer-to-peer network was quickly installed, with an Internet connection and an email server. Fiona provided good training and monitored results. Productivity increased and clients were pleased at being able to deal with the company by email.

PREDICTING FUTURE DEVELOPMENTS

Today's client/server systems are powerful but require the use of personal computers that are costly to maintain and hard to keep updated. Modern, fast networks based on Internet standards offer an alternative, lower-cost solution. Simple network computers (NCs) are linked to a very powerful server using a high-speed network. The NCs do not need a powerful processor or any internal hard discs for data storage, so they are cheap to build and maintain. They use a programming language called Java or a simple version of Windows, which enables them to control application programs based on a server. Because all computing activity takes place on the server, it is easy to control, but it needs a powerful server and a fast network.

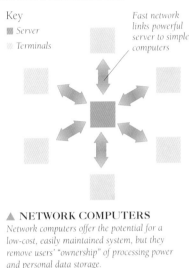

Key
■ Server
▨ Terminals

Fast network links powerful server to simple computers

▲ NETWORK COMPUTERS
Network computers offer the potential for a low-cost, easily maintained system, but they remove users' "ownership" of processing power and personal data storage.

ENSURING RELIABILITY

Large networks are quite complicated and require specialized skills to set up and manage them. A network administrator is usually responsible for ensuring the system runs efficiently. Speed and reliability are key factors. A slow network reduces efficiency, and any failure can bring work to a complete halt. Get a specialist to check your network if it does not give 99 percent reliability, or if it slows significantly under heavy traffic.

36 Explore the potential benefits of using the Java language to run network applications from a server.

FOCUSING ON SOFTWARE

As a manager you must be able to use a selection of software programs, many of which have become standard management productivity tools. You should be familiar with common programs, know how to select software, and understand your staff's needs.

37 Let others be the first to experiment with new software on the market.

CHOOSING SOFTWARE

In large organizations, decisions about software may be made by an IT department; in others, you will have some freedom to choose software that suits your needs. Always take time to select software carefully: it is often expensive and takes time to learn, so choosing inappropriately can be an expensive mistake. If software is chosen by others and you feel you need new tools, research possible alternatives, then make your case.

38 Choose widely used software for best compatibility when sharing data.

COMMON SOFTWARE TOOLS

TYPE OF SOFTWARE	KEY POINTS
OPERATING SYSTEM Software that controls the computer, all inputs and outputs, and the user interface.	Modern operating systems such as Windows, Linux, and MacOS use an icon-based, graphical user interface (GUI) to simplify working. Computers running different operating systems can communicate on a network.
APPLICATION SOFTWARE Accounting, desktop publishing, and graphic-design tools are examples of specific application programs.	Many managers have particular job requirements that demand expertise in specialized tools. Pick industry-leading programs, learn to use them well, and install any important upgrades to stay compatible with other users.
PRODUCTIVITY SOFTWARE Application software for standard office tasks such as word processing is often called productivity software.	Pick productivity software that allows you to use information from one program in another application. Thus, data from a spreadsheet can be inserted easily into a word-processor document, database, or presentation.

PINPOINTING MANAGEMENT SOFTWARE

The software you use at work will depend on the nature of your job and the type of organization, but most managers regularly use office productivity software. With the growth of the Internet, email and Web-browsing software are also commonly used. In addition, you may use powerful business-management software written for your specific industry, or specialist application software such as graphic, multimedia or design tools. Thorough training in all specialized software is essential if you are to get the best use out of it.

 39 Remember, 80 percent of users need only 20 percent of the features offered by most programs.

SELECTING SOFTWARE

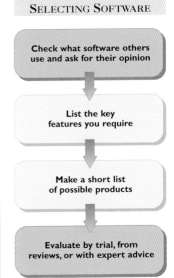

Check what software others use and ask for their opinion

List the key features you require

Make a short list of possible products

Evaluate by trial, from reviews, or with expert advice

USING A WORD PROCESSOR

Word processing is the most common software requirement for managers. In most cases, the needs are quite simple: to write and format a letter or report, for instance. Today's word processors have, however, almost the same features as professional desktop-publishing software and are far more feature-packed and complicated than most people require. Focus on fully learning only the features you use most often. Ignore those you rarely need. Important skills include formatting a document, saving a format as a template that can be re-used, and applying fonts and styles (such as bold and italics) to text.

MICROSOFT WORD ▼
Microsoft Word is the most commonly used word-processing software. With it, you can set up standard templates for letters, faxes, and memos.

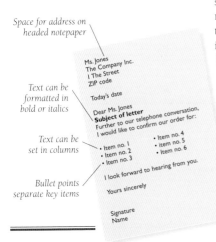

Space for address on headed notepaper

Text can be formatted in bold or italics

Text can be set in columns

Bullet points separate key items

Ms. Jones
The Company Inc.
I The Street
ZIP code

Today's date

Dear Ms. Jones
Subject of letter
Further to our telephone conversation, I would like to confirm our order for:

• Item no. I
• Item no. 2
• Item no. 3
• Item no. 4
• Item no. 5
• Item no. 6

I look forward to hearing from you.

Yours sincerely

Signature
Name

USING A SPREADSHEET

A spreadsheet program is potentially the most useful and powerful tool at a manager's disposal. A spreadsheet is a simple grid of cells arranged in rows and columns. Each cell can hold text, a number, or a formula, and users can create their own layout, define relationships between data, and devise formulas for calculations. You can also present the data in chart, table, or graph form. Spreadsheets are far less structured than most software but offer a very flexible tool for working with numbers and formulas. They are ideal for financial work or any other numerical calculation such as building sales forecasts or identifying cost or profit scenarios to answer "what if?" questions. The latest spreadsheets allow you to publish data on a Web or intranet site and share your data with your customers and suppliers.

POINTS TO REMEMBER

● Spreadsheet programs may seem daunting to learn, but they are important and powerful tools for analyzing data.

● More time will be spent mastering this software than most others.

● A wide range of graphical presentation styles is offered by modern spreadsheet programs, allowing complex information to be clearly presented.

● To save time formatting a spreadsheet, a template should be set up for calculations that are used regularly.

40 Make it a priority to learn how to use a spreadsheet.

VERSATILE SPREADSHEETS ▼
Learning to use a spreadsheet effectively enables you to organize, analyze, and present data—such as year-end results—in ways that suit your needs.

Quarter	01	02	03	04	Total
Seasonal adjustment	0.9	1.1	0.8	1.2	
Number Units Sold	5,644	6,898	5,017	7,525	25,084
Sales Revenue	214,467	262,126	190,637	285,956	953,186
Cost of Sales	124,165	151,757	110,369	165,553	551,844
Gross Margin	90,302	110,369	80,268	120,403	401,342
Sales costs	8,000	8,000	9,000	9,000	34,000
Advertising	10,000	10,000	10,000	10,000	40,000
Overhead	25,736	31,455	22,876	34,315	114,382
Total costs	43,736	49,455	41,876	53,315	188,382
Gross Profit	46,566	60,914	38,392	67,088	212,960
Profit Margin	22%	23%	20%	23%	22%

Create headings and rows, then enter data and formulas into cells

When a variable is changed, results can be calculated automatically

The most popular spreadsheets include Microsoft Excel and Lotus 1-2-3

Most spreadsheets can present data in charts, tables, or graphical form

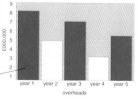

£000,000

year 1　year 2　year 3　year 4　year 5
overheads

First Name	Last Name	Address	ZIP Code	Telephone
James	Talbot	15 Moonshill Road	80303	303-123-4567
Jonathon	Dean	306 Hastings Drive	08077	609-891-2345
Joshua	Brown	Ash Lane	29708	803-678-9123

A record is a collection of items of information about one person or thing

A field is one element of the record: in this case, the client's last name

A table consists of a number of records. One or more tables make a database

ELEMENTS OF A DATABASE ▲
A database consists of one or more tables, each of which is made up of fields and records. By performing a search of the database, you can quickly locate information of specific interest—for instance, all clients living in a particular town.

WORKING WITH DATABASES

A spreadsheet is a useful tool for organizing lists of data, but when you need to manage large amounts of information, a database program is far more powerful. A database can be built to manage a mailing list, customer and supplier information, product details, employee payroll information, or any other information that requires collating, managing, and analyzing. In today's business environment, which focuses on information and knowledge management, databases are essential. Simple, "flat-file" databases give access only to the data stored in that database, but a "relational" database allows you to define relationships between two or more databases. This gives you a powerful tool for finding, sorting, and analyzing information stored in different databases.

43 Unless you have specialized needs, choose a ready-made program rather than a custom one.

41 Increase availability of data by linking several databases.

42 Create standard reports for the information you need regularly.

THINGS TO DO

1. Consider how you wish to use and present the data once the database is in use.

2. Plan your database on paper before building it on screen.

3. List all the fields you want to include in the database.

4. Identify any necessary relationships between separate databases.

MAKING A PRESENTATION

*P*resentation software can make the task
of producing a presentation relatively
quick and easy, and it offers new ways of
distributing information. Practice is needed
to master the software, however, and some
design skills are required for best results.

44 Take notice of the ways others create presentations and learn from them.

THINGS TO DO

1. Be clear about the type and frequency of presentations you need to produce.

2. Discuss your needs with colleagues and get advice on software and techniques.

3. Allow plenty of time to learn new software.

4. Practice with the software before you need to use it.

5. Use specialized designers for important or complex, interactive presentations.

CHOOSING THE RIGHT PRESENTATION PACKAGE

Before you pick a software program to use, you must consider the type of presentations you plan to produce. A simple presentation may require only paper handouts and overhead projection transparencies, but a major event could call for video, audio, animation, and transition effects. Think about whether you want to produce 35mm slides or display the presentation from a laptop computer. You may need to create an interactive presentation for use on a website or DVD disc. Microsoft Powerpoint is a popular business presentation package; other, specialized programs, such as Macromedia Director, offer greater power and more flexibility, but demand greater expertise to exploit their features.

QUESTIONS TO ASK YOURSELF

Q Am I the right person to be producing these presentations?

Q Will I need to create presentations on a regular basis?

Q What kind of presentations will I need to produce?

Q How will I deliver the presentations – do I need to publish on the Web?

Q Is there a software program available in my organization?

Q Can I learn to use the program or do I need a specialist?

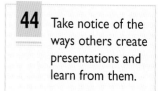

45 Distribute interactive presentations on CD-ROM, by email, or on a website.

CREATING A GOOD PRESENTATION

Just because a software program provides many features, it does not mean you should use them all. This is very true of presentation software, which typically gives you the option of selecting from a wide range of styles, effects, and transitions. Unless you are a professional designer, the best advice is to keep it simple:

● Use a clear layout that does not distract from the content of your presentation.
● Use graphics, video, and audio for impact, but do not overuse animated effects and transitions.

 46 Minimize text by making use of bullet points.

 **47** Choose graphics to help communicate your message in a clear way.

◀ MAKING AN IMPACT
Remember that simplicity and clarity are likely to have greatest impact. Avoid messy or confusing effects that distract the audience.

POINTS TO REMEMBER

● All graphics and text should be prepared before the building of the presentation is started.
● Audience handouts should be produced to enhance an on-screen presentation.
● Alternative means of delivering an electronic presentation should be arranged in case of problems.
● Interactive material can be used effectively on your website to inform and entertain customers.

AVOIDING PROBLEMS

Remember that complex and important presentations require significant time and skill to create, and entail the possibility of things going wrong. Avoid getting carried away by the abilities of the technology and focus on the importance of the audience. Ensure that the content, style, and sophistication of the presentation are appropriate to the messages you are trying to relay. Allow plenty of time to build the presentation, and make time for a practice run at the location, using the same equipment that you will use on the day.

MANAGING EMAIL

Email provides a cheap, fast, and efficient means of sending electronic messages around the office or around the world. The ease of sending messages can cause problems, so you and your staff must learn when and how best to use email.

48 If you send a very urgent email, use the telephone to warn the recipient.

49 Pick up your email when you are on the move by using the latest mobile phone technology.

RUNNING EMAIL

An email program lets you create, receive, store, and manage your messages. Popular programs include Microsoft Outlook, Qualcomm Eudora Pro, and Netscape Communicator. The best way to run email in an organization is to use a network server to manage internal email and control a permanent, or dial-up, Internet connection. If you have a permanent or regular, periodic connection, email will arrive automatically at each computer on the network. Otherwise, it is kept at the ISP until you dial in and collect it.

HOW EMAIL WORKS ▼
Email is sent to your Internet Service Provider (ISP) and then, via Internet mail servers, to the recipient's ISP.

Sender writes a message using email program

Mail routed across the Internet

Mail server at recipient's ISP receives mail

Mail server at sender's ISP receives mail and forwards it

Recipient receives mail, often within seconds

USING EMAIL EFFICIENTLY

Today, email is an increasingly important tool, but if used poorly it can be a time-waster and a cause of irritation. It is vital to ensure that you and your staff thoroughly learn how to use your email program.

- Use a modern email program for maximum compatibility with other email users.
- Learn how to add file attachments to messages.
- Organize your messages into folders, and regularly delete or archive old messages.
- Take as much care composing an email as you would a letter.

POINTS TO REMEMBER

- Your organization should have an email use policy – make sure you know and follow its instructions.
- The assumption should never be made that a message has been read – some people do not check their mailboxes regularly.
- If an email you sent is returned to you (called "bouncing") it is likely you addressed it incorrectly.
- Email is not a secure form of communication. A message may be read by someone other than the intended recipient.
- An encryption program should be used to keep important email messages secure, but discuss this with your IT staff first.

DO'S AND DON'TS

✔ Do deal with incoming emails quickly and file important messages.

✔ Do delete "junk" mail unread or use a filter in your program to discard it automatically.

✔ Do learn to use reply and forward features in your email program.

✔ Do keep messages and any attachments as small as possible.

✘ DON'T WRITE IN CAPITALS. It is called "shouting" and can cause offense.

✘ Don't automatically include all recipients of an original message in your reply.

✘ Don't use rude or profane language.

✘ Don't use your business email address for personal messages.

50 Use your email address book feature to organize contact details and create groups of contacts.

AVOIDING PROBLEMS

Most of the problems users have with email stem from misunderstanding or misuse. Many organizations implement email systems without sufficient training for staff and without considering the implications of this latest form of written communication. Because email is quick and easy to write, it can be used indiscriminately. Tell staff to check before sending an email that it is really necessary and that there is not a more appropriate way to communicate. They should write clearly and concisely, and take trouble to ensure that spelling, grammar, and punctuation are correct. Remember that laws such as those dealing with libel and contract issues apply to email as much as other written forms. A great deal of damage can be done by a carelessly written message or a sensitive note sent to the wrong recipient.

USING THE WEB

The World Wide Web is just one part of the Internet, but its rich graphical presentation has made it the most popular and fastest-growing area. The Web is an increasingly important business resource, so learning how to explore and use it is vital.

51 Upgrade your browser to make use of the latest Web features.

CULTURAL DIFFERENCES

The Internet is a global medium that in many ways transcends conventional, national, and cultural boundaries. Because it was American organizations and individuals that first took up use of the Internet, English is the principal language, but as usage spreads and cultural variety increases, we can expect to see an increase in sites in all other languages.

52 Pick the browser that feels the most intuitive to use.

EXPLORING A WORLD ▶ OF INFORMATION
The Web is an invaluable resource for fast research into new suppliers, including services such as corporate training, client entertainment, and overseas travel.

STARTING ON THE WEB

The Web uses a programming language called HyperText Markup Language (HTML) and a transmission standard called HyperText Transfer Protocol (HTTP). HTML allows the publication of "pages" containing text, graphics, video, and audio files. It also allows any element on a page to be linked to any other page on the Web. A website consists of a collection of pages published by an individual or organization. It is stored on a Web server connected to the Internet. Using a Web browser program on your computer, you connect to the Internet and request a page on the Web, which is then delivered by the server that holds it.

USING A BROWSER

The HTML language is constantly evolving as new features are added to improve the Web's ability to display multimedia (text, graphics, audio, and video) content, and to enhance the presentation of information. Web browsers are updated frequently, so make sure you use the latest upgrade for your chosen browser. Microsoft Internet Explorer and Netscape Navigator are the two most popular browsers, and both are free to download from the Web. Browsers are easy to use, and offer features that can save time while "surfing" (exploring websites). Use the "Favorites" or "Bookmarks" feature to save addresses of favorite Web pages, and the "History" feature to find sites you visited recently.

BEING SECURITY AWARE

Contrary to popular perception, security for online financial transactions is high, and potentially safer than most traditional means of paying by credit card. There are, however, real security issues to consider:

- Encode sensitive email information by using an encryption program.
- Be aware that a Web server can track your movements and can identify certain information about you.
- Financial transactions should be carried out on an encrypted, secure server. Most browsers show a padlock in the status bar to indicate when a secure connections exists.

http:// tells the browser to look for a hypertext document

Most, but not all, Web addresses have www. as the next part of the address

Dots (.) separate the elements of the Web address

The final part loosely indicates the type of organization

http://www.dk.com

There are no spaces in a Web address

dk.com is the domain name of the organization that owns this site

"com" is used for a company, "org" for a non-profit organization, and "edu" for an educational institution

A WEB ADDRESS ▲
In order for a Web browser to find a single page among the millions on the Web, each page is given a unique address

53 To speed up page downloading, turn off graphic loading.

UNDERSTANDING WEB ADDRESSES

Every Web page has a unique address called a Uniform Resource Locator (URL), which describes the location of the server where it is stored. For instance, www.dk.com is the address for the home (starting) page of Dorling Kindersley's website. In fact, though Web addresses start with http://, a modern browser does not need you to type this.

PICKING OTHER SOFTWARE

In addition to the main software tools that most managers encounter, there are many others that you may need, or choose to use. Make sure that your basic business needs are met before considering other programs that can help you to be more efficient.

 54 Wait to buy new software for 3–6 months after it is first released.

 55 Always ensure that your data is backed up on a frequent basis.

PICKING USEFUL TOOLS

If your computer is maintained by IT staff you should discuss software options with them, and avoid installing programs without their knowledge. Otherwise, do some research, ask colleagues for their advice, and test out trial versions before buying programs. Use the Internet to research software and download trial copies.

ADDITIONAL BUSINESS SOFTWARE TOOLS

SOFTWARE	BENEFITS
DATA BACKUP	Crucial for peace of mind, backup software runs on a network or individual PCs to make copies of your data.
COMPRESSION TOOLS	These compress and decompress files for transmission over the Internet or to increase disk storage capacity.
PC & NETWORK MONITORING	PC and network analysis tools monitor PC and network performance, and are used to spot and solve problems.
SECURITY SYSTEMS	Security programs can control access to data on PCs, or to resources on a network, an intranet, or the Internet.
VOICE RECOGNITION & SPEECH	These useful business tools allow you to control the computer by voice and enable it to speak to you.
GRAPHICS PRODUCTION	Graphic tools allow you to produce literature, multimedia programs, and presentations quickly and cost effectively.

USING BUSINESS MANAGEMENT SYSTEMS

Business management systems are designed to integrate many or all of the main organizational functions (such as accounting, manufacturing, sales, supply ordering, and distribution) within a single system that is used to run and manage the entire business. These systems are usually designed for specific industry needs, and they use powerful databases to store and manipulate the corporate data. They are often very expensive to implement, and users must be involved in their design if they are to be successful. Users must also be given sufficient training in how to use the system.

56 Involve users when planning important computer systems.

> ### CASE STUDY
> The board of a medium-sized manufacturing company decided to upgrade the computer systems that managed their transaction processing. The existing systems did not communicate with one another, so information from the sales system had to be reentered into the accounting and distribution systems. The re-keying of data at least three times for each order caused delays, errors, and costs. The systems were incompatible with emerging Internet standards. The decision-makers decided to implement a full business-management system and insisted that it be able to share information across the corporate intranet and the Internet. Sales staff were able to enter orders from their laptops while with customers, and the system then managed the sales data through each stage of the business process.

GETTING IT RIGHT ▶
Implementing or upgrading business management software can have a major impact. Managed properly, it can deliver significant productivity improvements.

POINTS TO REMEMBER

- Successfully implementing a business management system can be one of the hardest challenges facing an organization.

- Ample time must be allowed for planning and consultation.

- The business process must be reviewed from start to finish, with the help of those who operate it, and any improvements made, before it is computerized.

SELECTING CUSTOM SOLUTIONS

Some business management systems are available "off-the-shelf," but the wide variety of different business models means that many organizations have to pay developers to modify a "standard" system to suit their individual needs. If a system has to be modified considerably, it will greatly increase the costs and complexity of the project. There is also an increased risk of major cost or time overruns, or even outright failure. Beware of completely custom projects, where a new system is developed from scratch, as these are notoriously difficult to manage. In all cases, have a clear and detailed contract with your supplier.

MANAGING IT

The importance of IT brings with it new requirements for managers. As well as being an able user of IT, you must be ready to manage the impact of technology on your staff.

PREPARING STAFF FOR IT

The most common reason for the failure of IT projects to deliver their potential benefits is lack of attention paid to the people who must work with the technology. It is essential to encourage staff to adopt IT, seek training, and use good working practices.

57 Maximize the benefits of IT by encouraging your team to embrace it.

QUESTIONS TO ASK YOURSELF

Q Do I take the importance of IT seriously enough?

Q Do I involve my team in decisions about IT systems?

Q Have I ensured that all my staff have been fully trained in the software they use?

Q Have my staff been trained in health and safety issues?

Q Do we have guidelines for the use of email and the Web?

EMPOWERING YOUR TEAM

People who are asked to use new technology are often reluctant to do so. This can surprise the designers of new systems, who tend to focus on technology rather than the people who will use the systems. Avoid problems by involving your team in all decisions about any IT system that affects them. Encourage users to think about ways in which IT can help with their work. Discuss IT developments with your staff, and empower them to suggest ways of improving performance. Lead by example, and point out that IT proficiency offers personal, as well as professional, benefits.

BEING AWARE OF HEALTH AND SAFETY ISSUES

Working at a computer for long periods of time can lead to some discomfort or health problems if attention is not paid to posture, workspace arrangement, and taking regular breaks. It is important to:

- Arrange your desk and chair so that you can sit comfortably and have enough space for a keyboard and mouse.
- Use an adjustable chair that gives firm support to your lower back.
- Position the monitor so that the top of the screen is at eye level.
- Adjust the distance of the screen from your eyes for personal comfort.
- Make sure that the screen is positioned to minimize glare or reflections.
- Use an adjustable monitor on a tilting stand so that you can easily adjust its position.
- Take frequent breaks, stand up and stretch, or walk around to ease tired muscles.
- Relax eye muscles by looking up from the screen regularly. Look into the distance, and blink often.

▼ CORRECT POSTURE
Adopt a good posture when working at a keyboard to avoid muscle and eye strain. Position the mouse within easy reach.

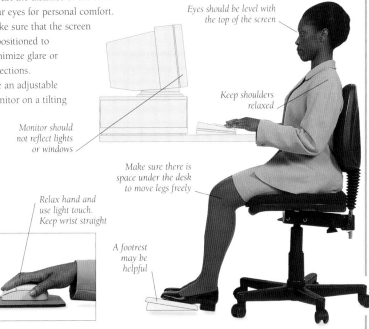

Eyes should be level with the top of the screen

Keep shoulders relaxed

Monitor should not reflect lights or windows

Make sure there is space under the desk to move legs freely

Relax hand and use light touch. Keep wrist straight

A footrest may be helpful

BREAKING DOWN RESISTANCE

An investment in technology can be largely wasted if users are not given sufficient training to use it effectively and to be proficient with new software. A common mistake is to assume that people are eager to learn new skills; but users may feel threatened by new technology or fail to see any personal benefits in training. Be sure to explain the reasons for using new technology, and create a business culture that encourages staff to increase their IT skills.

▼ TRAINING COURSES

Learning in a group situation with a good trainer can be an effective way to master new programs, especially if the course can be tailored to any specific needs that your staff may have.

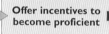

| Explain the benefits of taking training | Offer incentives to become proficient | Give good training and monitor results |

HELPING YOUR TEAM LEARN ▲

Managers frequently make the assumption that staff will readily take up training when it is provided. This is often not the case, and you may need to win them over to the idea.

DO'S AND DON'TS

✔ Do listen to users and ask them to define their training needs.

✔ Do make proficiency in using IT systems part of regular staff assessment.

✔ Do assess training providers carefully before selecting training courses.

✘ Don't arrange training before discussing needs with staff.

✘ Don't schedule training courses without checking users' availability.

✘ Don't assume that an off-the-shelf course will be suitable for all your staff equally.

 58 For best results from a training course, keep each session short.

 59 Encourage proficient staff to learn how to help the less skilled.

PICKING A TRAINING METHOD

METHODS	PROS	CONS
LEARNING BY USING	This can be the quickest method for staff experienced in similar programs.	This can be slow and very difficult for inexperienced or reluctant computer users.
USING THE MANUAL	A good manual will help experienced computer users solve problems as they learn.	Many manuals are poorly written and confuse inexperienced users.
SPECIALIZED BOOKS	Many books dealing with specialized programs are much better than the manual.	Many are very large, seem daunting, and can confuse novices more than they help.
TRAINING COURSES	Organized training courses with good teachers are often a good way to learn quickly.	These may be expensive, and require staff to be away from the office for several days.
IN-HOUSE TRAINING	This can provide flexible learning for small groups, with lessons based on their need.	This is more expensive than out-of-house training courses and needs more organization.
ONLINE AND CD-BASED	The best programs are very flexible and are effective for self-motivated learners.	This requires multimedia PCs. Users need to put time and effort into solo learning.

ORGANIZING TRAINING

Many users have very specific requirements from their software, and only rarely need to understand all the features of a package. Focus training for most users on the parts of the package they need to use all the time, and have just one or two team members trained in the features that are used less frequently. If possible, arrange training in-house rather than at a training establishment, and ask the trainer to tailor the course to suit your requirements. After initial training, make further courses available as needed, and ensure that users know how to get help if they encounter problems.

THINGS TO DO

1. Discuss training with users.
2. Research the options for training, and ask others for referrals and references.
3. Sit in on a similar course before picking a trainer.
4. Make sure that users have all the details of the training course well in advance.

Helping Your Staff Avoid Problems

In order to help your staff avoid problems you should publish guidelines for using IT resources, especially email and the Web. Encourage staff to keep up to date with IT and provide ways for them to do so. Inform staff if their use of IT resources is monitored.

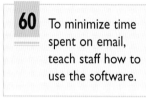

60 To minimize time spent on email, teach staff how to use the software.

Setting Web Use Policy

When staff are first given access to the Web it is normal for individuals to spend quite some time exploring sites and learning about the Web. This is to be encouraged, but guidelines should set parameters to prevent time-wasting online, and to prohibit visits to inappropriate sites. You will probably wish to limit the downloading of software to a network administrator, to reduce the risk from viruses. You should also use server software to bar entry to inappropriate sites, and to monitor, and log, use of the Web by your staff.

Setting Email Policy

Far too many companies implement the use of email without providing appropriate guidelines. An organization should have clear rules for using email, and should ensure that all staff receive full training in using it efficiently. Guidelines should specify that all email belongs to the organization, that staff use can be monitored, and that all saved emails are archived as part of the organization's record keeping. The legal status of email should be explained, and guidance should be given on what is considered acceptable personal use.

61 Ask staff to keep personal email use to a minimum.

62 Learn how to use filtering tools in email software.

KEEPING STAFF AWARE

The rapid developments taking place in IT will have significant business impact. If opportunities are to be identified, it is important to encourage your key staff to keep up with the speed of change. Suggest they focus on technologies that are important to your business, and on new developments in the software you use. A regular check should also be kept on wider developments, especially those offering faster network speed and wireless communication.

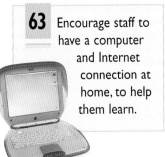

63 Encourage staff to have a computer and Internet connection at home, to help them learn.

Talks to IT-literate staff regularly and shows interest in the subject

Skims computer or Internet periodicals occasionally

Subscribes to Internet mailing lists covering IT for managers

Reads technology ages in newspapers and magazines

Has a computer for home use and surfs the Web

◀ **KEEPING UP**
Remember that it is important for your career to understand the benefits to be obtained from technology both for your staff and for your business. Develop your own preferred strategies for keeping up with developments, and encourage your staff to work on the same principles.

DO'S AND DON'TS

✔ Do help staff to keep up to date with new developments in IT.

✔ Do have guidelines for using computers, network resources, and the Internet.

✔ Do discuss use of monitoring with staff and draw up agreed guidelines.

✗ Don't expect staff to want to learn to use new technology.

✗ Don't be impatient with staff who take time to learn to use new technology.

✗ Don't forget to create a forum for staff to discuss technology and make suggestions.

MONITORING YOUR STAFF

The technology that helps your staff to communicate easily and quickly also makes it possible to monitor their use of the technology. Monitoring staff to the extent allowed by the latest systems has ethical and practical implications and should not be done without staff being informed. Remember that monitoring without a clear purpose is pointless, takes human and network resources, and could easily lower morale.

REVIEWING THE BUSINESS PROCESS

An organization's business process often evolves over time, to suit changes in the company or its marketplace. It is essential to review the process and make it as efficient as possible before implementing IT solutions to support it.

64 Start by assuming that there is a better way of doing things.

65 Listen to your customers and your staff to find new opportunities.

POINTS TO REMEMBER

- A process is not necessarily effective just because "it has always been done this way."
- A business process is liable to become static and inflexible, while business needs can change rapidly.
- IT issues must not be considered until the best scenario for the business process has been devised.
- Top-performing competitors should be benchmarked.

ANALYZING THE ▶ SITUATION
Try looking at your organization with a fresh eye, and consider every part of your business process to find ways to improve it.

ANALYZING THE CURRENT SITUATION

In today's fast-changing world, it is not unusual to find that parts of your business process have become unnecessary or inefficient since they were first implemented. Many organizations are now choosing to outsource parts of the process as they redefine their core business skills. Before implementing any major IT solution, always start by reevaluating your current business process. Check that the business strategy has not changed since the existing process was created.

Considers whether business needs have changed

Benchmarks competitors to test for new alternatives

REDEFINING THE BUSINESS PROCESS

Once you have analyzed the current situation, you should create a "wish list" that describes your ideal business process. Make sure you have a good IT strategist in your team to advise on the capabilities of technology, but do not consider specific IT tools at this stage. Give users a "blue skies" scenario to find their ideal process. Involve suppliers and customers, if possible, in order to develop the most effective business process.

66 Look outside your own industry for good ideas your business can use.

CASE STUDY
A leading car distributor needed to update its aging transaction processing system. First, however, decision-makers decided to conduct a full review of the marketplace and the existing business process. They reviewed the long-term strategy, and then asked staff working in the core process for ideas to make the process more efficient. Customers and suppliers were involved in the review, and a wish list of needs was drawn up. Ideas on how to use IT to improve the process were put forward, but the process redesign was not limited by planning for specific software. The company looked outside its industry and identified the Internet as being of increasing importance, so it decided to require Internet compatibility for all software. Finally, potential suppliers were briefed on requirements, and a successful bidder was selected.

THE BEST ▶ WAY FORWARD
Reviewing business strategy and core processes is time-consuming but necessary when significant IT expenditure is considered.

PLANNING AN IT SOLUTION

Agree the business process with management and users

⬇

List all requirements for an IT system to handle the process

⬇

Work with IT staff to evaluate potential solutions

⬇

Ensure users accept chosen system and give full training

DESIGNING A SOLUTION

Once you have redefined your strategy, examined your existing process, and decided on changes that may be needed, you are ready to discuss specific IT solutions with potential suppliers. Using the analysis of your ideal process, produce a specification describing the results that a new system must be able to deliver. Do not specify how the software should deliver the results; leave suppliers free to suggest alternative approaches that you may not have considered. Remember to specify the existing systems with which a new one must communicate, and insist that new software be Internet-compatible, to allow you to share information easily with others.

PLANNING RESOURCES

In order to plan the resources you will require in the future, you have to imagine how your organization will need to work in an increasingly Internet-dominated world. You must focus on creating a seamless process that is targeted at meeting customers' needs.

67 Use improved productivity as your key test for new resources.

68 Plan on doing more and more business online.

LOOKING TO THE FUTURE

The pace of change in information technology is now so rapid that planning the resources you will need, even for the next year or two, can be very difficult. Although it is impossible to predict the future fully, you should spend some time trying to imagine your business in two or three years' time, and consider how you wish to be doing business in the future. Focus on how many people you expect to be using your IT systems, and what kind of services your customers require. Pay special attention to conducting business via the Internet.

LOOKING AHEAD ▼
When planning IT resources, you need to examine the current position, take note of staff suggestions, and then look ahead, always focusing on working effectively with suppliers and customers.

Aims for efficient sharing of customer and supplier information

Works toward sharing databases internally, and with suppliers and customers

Listens to users' suggestions or requests for better tools

Ensures systems and tools work with online suppliers and customers

Establishes how up-to-date current systems and tools are

Checks systems are as effective as those of competitors

IDENTIFYING YOUR NEEDS

Start by asking your customers and suppliers for comments on the process of doing business with you and look for ways in which IT can improve the customer and supplier relationships. Work with your staff to identify the pros and cons of existing systems. If possible, research how your main competitors are using IT to improve their performance, and look at other industries for new ideas. Look for software tools that can deliver the results you want, then decide on hardware needs.

QUESTIONS TO ASK YOURSELF

Q Have I taken the time to look at my business from my customers' point of view?

Q Do I accept the need to turn my organization into an online business for future success?

Q Have I taken into account the views of my staff, and allowed for their different needs?

POINTS TO REMEMBER

- For most organizations, adopting the Internet as a major business tool should not be thought of as an option – it is essential.

- A fast internal network and a fast and reliable Internet connection must be considered as absolutely vital to future plans.

- Considerable growth in network traffic should be allowed for when your network needs are being planned.

MOVING TO E-BUSINESS

The development of the Internet has changed business forever. Organizations that were quick to realize the commercial implications have focused on developing IT systems compatible with Internet standards, so as to ensure effective use of the medium. Many businesses are adapting to e-commerce (the process of selling goods and services online) but this is only a part of the transformation into an e-business, in which all the organization's processes and systems are integrated to provide seamless and transparent service.

ALLOWING FOR VARIETY

Remember that different groups of staff will have vastly different information and computing needs. Some will only require reliable network access to databases with simple, effective tools for data input. Others may need powerful computers, and graphic or design software, together with a high capacity network to allow for fast transfer of very large files. Marketeers and after-sales staff will require quick access to customer and product databases and analytical tools. Most staff will benefit from a good intranet through which they can easily access the company's information pool.

69 Look at other industries for their view of the future.

70 Build flexibility into your systems to allow for changing needs.

WORKING WITH IT STAFF

The relationship between IT staff and the rest of the organization is an important element in using technology successfully. IT services must be focused on delivering real business benefit, and IT users should be encouraged to assess the service they receive.

71 Pick staff for IT services who can communicate well with users.

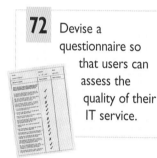

72 Devise a questionnaire so that users can assess the quality of their IT service.

ASSESSING THE IT SERVICE

IT staff are too often seen as a separate part of an organization and are sometimes considered to be difficult to communicate with. A good IT service understands business issues and provides strategic IT advice at senior level. It delivers high-quality systems, training, and support services to users, and communicates effectively. Evaluate IT staff by consulting non-IT staff on the quality of service, and by comparing costs with external suppliers.

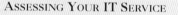

ASSESSING YOUR IT SERVICE

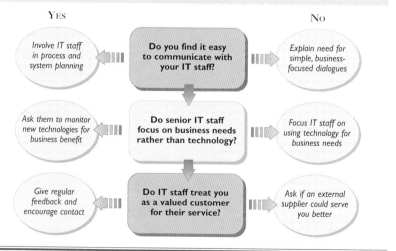

YES   No

Involve IT staff in process and system planning ◁ **Do you find it easy to communicate with your IT staff?** ▷ Explain need for simple, business-focused dialogues

Ask them to monitor new technologies for business benefit ◁ **Do senior IT staff focus on business needs rather than technology?** ▷ Focus IT staff on using technology for business needs

Give regular feedback and encourage contact ◁ **Do IT staff treat you as a valued customer for their service?** ▷ Ask if an external supplier could serve you better

FOCUSING ON BUSINESS REQUIREMENTS

If an organization is to get the best out of IT, it must involve senior IT staff in business decision-making and focus them on using technology not for its own sake but to deliver specific business benefits. An organization should have a senior person who is sufficiently knowledgeable in IT, as well as the business strategy, to be able to advise at board level on the implications of emerging technologies. IT staff should work closely with managers and users in all departments to ensure that the IT function is fully integrated into the organization's operations. The staff who provide support services to users, manage systems, and organize training must have good communication skills in order to provide top-quality assistance.

THINGS TO DO

1. Examine the quality of the IT service you receive.
2. Involve your team in assessing IT performance.
3. Seek to build better relationships with IT specialists.
4. Explain the business needs behind requests you make for IT services.
5. Involve IT staff in business project teams.
6. Give feedback to IT staff.

BUILDING RELATIONSHIPS

It is quite common for staff to feel intimidated by IT experts and to find it difficult to ask for help or advice. Look for ways to bring together IT staff and users of the technology. Use formal and informal situations to develop links and build relationships. Arrange sessions to explain the importance of IT to users, and the needs of the business to IT staff.

A GOOD WORKING RELATIONSHIP ▲
The effective use of IT is now so important for commercial success that it is essential to build good working relationships between IT staff and other parts of the organization.

73 Motivate IT staff to focus on the real needs.

WORKING WITH CONSULTANTS

Consultants are an important part of many IT projects, since they provide skills and experience not available in-house. Costs can be high, however, so it is vital that you understand when to employ them and how to manage the working relationship.

74 Always define specific objectives when employing consultants.

APPOINTING A CONSULTANT

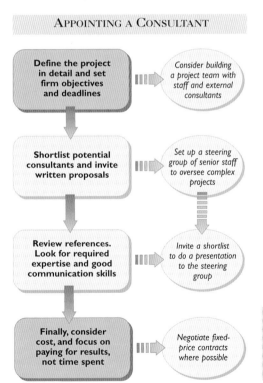

Define the project in detail and set firm objectives and deadlines
→ *Consider building a project team with staff and external consultants*

Shortlist potential consultants and invite written proposals
→ *Set up a steering group of senior staff to oversee complex projects*

Review references. Look for required expertise and good communication skills
→ *Invite a shortlist to do a presentation to the steering group*

Finally, consider cost, and focus on paying for results, not time spent
→ *Negotiate fixed-price contracts where possible*

WHEN TO USE A CONSULTANT

There are several situations in which you should consider employing consultants. At the strategic level, an independent and objective viewpoint can be very useful, even if you have a good understanding of the value of IT. At the operational level, a consultant may offer specific skills or experience not available in-house. The implementation phase of a new project is often one for which specialized skills are needed for a limited time, and the use of consultants is usually more appropriate than employing extra in-house staff.

75 Try to ensure the transfer of useful skills to your staff.

SELECTING A CONSULTANT

Before starting the selection process make sure you have clearly defined the project, its objectives, the timeline, and the results expected from consultants. If the project affects more than one part of your organization, form a steering group to oversee the project. Members should be drawn from senior managers representing the departments affected by the project. Prepare a consultancy brief and research a shortlist of suitable consultants. Invite a small number to make a presentation to the steering group and review references.

▼ MEETING THE CONSULTANT

When choosing a consultant, check technical, personal, and communication details before considering price.

76 Make sure that consultants are able to be productive by providing any information they need on time.

DO'S AND DON'TS

✔ Do use a project team approach that brings together in-house staff and consultants.	✘ Don't employ consultants on open-ended contracts without agreed aims and objectives.
✔ Do define the roles and responsibilities of consultants and in-house staff.	✘ Don't relinquish control once you have appointed consultants.
✔ Do use a steering group of senior managers to guide and monitor the project to its conclusion.	✘ Don't use consultants for tasks that can be done by in-house staff more cost-effectively

MANAGING THE RELATIONSHIP

A project manager should be appointed to take control of the assignment and manage the relationships with consultants on a day-to-day basis. For long projects, in particular, aim to develop good relationships between key team members and encourage informal contact. Hold regular review sessions with members of the project team and refer to the objectives and key deadlines to keep the project on track. Quickly resolve any difficulties between your in-house staff and consultants, and do not allow minor problems to escalate into serious friction.

OUTSOURCING IT

Today, outsourcing part or all of an organization's IT function is becoming increasingly popular. It can be a sensible approach if it delivers high-quality services at lower cost than in-house resources, but it requires careful assessment and management.

77 Consider letting your own IT department bid for contracts.

POINTS TO REMEMBER

- A business activity might be of strategic importance, but the IT function that supports it need not be, and could be outsourced.
- Vital flexibility will be lost if you pick a single supplier or agree long-term contracts.
- Consideration should be given to outsourcing the whole function, rather than the IT systems (for example, the payroll function).
- Your flexibility will be increased by competition for contracts between suppliers, including your IT department.

CONSIDERING THE BENEFITS AND THE RISKS

Outsourcing can be an attractive option because, in theory, it gives access to market-leading skills and technology while delivering savings on the IT budget. One problem, however, is that if outsourcing is not handled correctly, it may limit your organization's flexibility and control over its direction. In order to decide if outsourcing is of benefit, you should look at each of your IT systems in turn and consider whether cost savings could be achieved without restricting flexibility. Decide whether a system is of strategic value to your business (few are), of business-critical importance, or of a basic service nature.

NEGOTIATING CONTRACTS

When selecting potential outsourcing partners, and negotiating contracts, it is very important to avoid handing over too much power to one supplier. If you are planning to outsource several systems, draw up a shortlist of potential suppliers and seek individual bids for each service. If you do not have experience in outsourcing contracts, appoint a consultant and an IT contract lawyer to assist you. Examine each bid carefully and look for the "hidden extras" with which suppliers aim to earn extra profit from you.

78 Agree only to short contracts, with strict performance targets and penalty clauses.

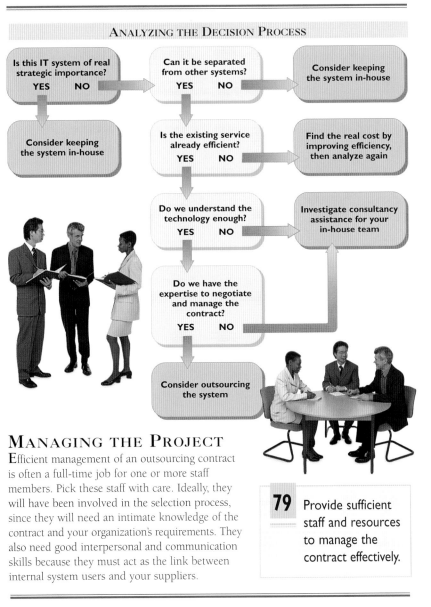

ANALYZING THE DECISION PROCESS

Is this IT system of real strategic importance?
YES   NO ▶

Can it be separated from other systems?
YES   NO ▶

Consider keeping the system in-house

Consider keeping the system in-house

Is the existing service already efficient?
YES   NO ▶

Find the real cost by improving efficiency, then analyze again

Do we understand the technology enough?
YES   NO ▶

Investigate consultancy assistance for your in-house team

Do we have the expertise to negotiate and manage the contract?
YES   NO

Consider outsourcing the system

MANAGING THE PROJECT

Efficient management of an outsourcing contract is often a full-time job for one or more staff members. Pick these staff with care. Ideally, they will have been involved in the selection process, since they will need an intimate knowledge of the contract and your organization's requirements. They also need good interpersonal and communication skills because they must act as the link between internal system users and your suppliers.

79 Provide sufficient staff and resources to manage the contract effectively.

53

PROFITING FROM THE INTERNET

The Internet is the most significant business development since the Industrial Revolution. Managers must assimilate the huge changes it is creating if their businesses are to succeed.

A BUSINESS REVOLUTION

The Internet is enabling and driving unique opportunities and new markets. Yet for many organizations it also poses a real threat. You must quickly learn how to use the Internet more effectively than your competitors if you are to stay ahead.

80 Make it a priority to learn how to use the Internet for business.

81 Think about a global market for your products.

82 Use the Internet to reach niche markets and build relationships.

REALIZING THE POTENTIAL

The Internet is at least as significant as the invention of the printing press, the telephone, or the television. It has already brought immense change to the business world. Some companies will benefit from the changes, but many will not. Those who cannot react fast enough to competition and changing markets will find their existence seriously threatened by the Internet. Make it a priority to learn how to use the Internet for your business. Concentrate on ways to use the Internet for research, speeding business with your suppliers, and getting closer to your customers.

USEFUL PARTS OF THE INTERNET

PART	USE
EMAIL	Email is an essential tool for most businesses because it is the most efficient way of sending messages very quickly and cheaply. Documents or graphics can be attached to an email message, saving courier or postal service charges.
WORLD WIDE WEB	Another essential tool, the Web offers access to a world of information that can help organizations reduce their costs and develop individual relationships with their customers. The Web is also a vital business research tool.
NEWSGROUPS	Newsgroups can be very useful for conducting customer research or for keeping up to date with industry news. Newsgroup users post messages for others to read and respond to. Most email programs also read newsgroups.
MAILING LISTS	Mailing lists covering thousands of specialized topics are available by email. Many websites offer their users regular updates of information by email. Subscribe to mailing lists to research into products, customers, and IT.
CHAT ROOMS	Internet chat rooms allow people to congregate and "chat." Text typed on one keyboard can be seen on other users' screens. While public chat rooms have little business value, private ones can usefully be set up for meetings.
FTP (FILE TRANSFER PROTOCOL)	FTP allows files to be transferred to and from servers on the Internet, whatever type of computer you use. Modern Web browsers incorporate FTP ability. Much information and even software is freely available from FTP servers.
GOPHER	Gopher is another part of the Internet dedicated to finding information. It existed before (and has been largely eclipsed by) the World Wide Web, but it can be useful for finding specialized information not available on the Web.

CUTTING COSTS

The Internet is creating a ferociously competitive marketplace in many industries. Managers can use this to help cut their operating costs. Use the Web to cut the costs of communications and travel, and to get the best possible deals from suppliers.

83 Remember that the Internet puts power in the customer's hands.

POINTS TO REMEMBER

- The quality of Internet telephony was much poorer than the telephone system, but it is improving and is much cheaper.
- If you use a Wide Area Network with excess capacity, consider re-routing some of your internal phone calls and faxes across it.
- The Internet is in its early development period, but as bandwidth increases expect to use it for online conferences.
- Save costs by allowing staff to work at home with online access to the organization's intranet.

REDUCING YOUR COMMUNICATION COSTS

The Internet can be used to help cut business communication costs. Use email rather than faxes, mail, or couriers to send documents; and, if a large number of international faxes must still be sent, investigate Internet services that transmit faxes at lower cost than the telephone system. If you have a fast wide-area network connecting remote offices, explore online video-conferencing systems that can be effective enough to reduce the need for face-to-face meetings. Use your website and intranet to post answers to all those questions regularly asked by customers, suppliers, and staff, to save them from having to ask employees.

◀ **VIDEO-CONFERENCING ONLINE TO CUT COSTS**
With a fast network, you can save on travel costs by video-conferencing online with colleagues working at home or elsewhere in the country.

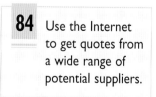

84 Use the Internet to get quotes from a wide range of potential suppliers.

REDUCING TRAVEL COSTS

The travel industry has been quick to exploit the Internet. It enables companies to offer last-minute deals and reduce the number of airline seats and hotel beds left empty, while providing excellent prices to customers. Use web travel sites to plan business travel, compare prices, and make sure you get the best discounts and frequent-flyer deals. Find the best deals quickly by using websites that compare prices across a number of airlines, hotels, car rental, and travel companies. Many of the best sites offer mailing-list services that inform you of last-minute deals.

THINGS TO DO

1. Research travel-related websites to find ones that are relevant to you.

2. Subscribe to mailing lists to stay informed.

3. Use travel-center sites that compare prices to find the best deals available.

4. Check deals and book online with your favorite airlines and hotels.

Uses the Internet to help recruit new staff

Looks for low-cost travel deals on-line

Shows staff how to cut costs using Internet resources

Looks for ways to cut communication and purchase costs

Uses the Internet to research new suppliers

◀ LOOKING FOR SAVINGS

As a manager, you should explore ways in which you can use the Web to make savings in cost areas that are significant to your organization, whatever its type and size. Your staff, too, must be educated in the potential savings.

CUTTING YOUR PURCHASE COSTS

The extraordinary growth in the Internet means that in many industries it is now possible to compare specifications, support services, and prices offered by a large number of suppliers. Indeed, there are websites that specialize in specific industries, putting you in touch with those suppliers that best match your needs. Whatever your requirements, use the Internet as a powerful research tool to reduce purchase costs.

85 Cut recruitment costs, and increase your reach, by recruiting via the Internet.

GETTING CLOSER TO THE CUSTOMER

The Internet allows you to reach a worldwide customer audience, whatever the size of your organization in the real world. Use it to get closer to your customers and provide a genuinely better service than that offered by your competitors.

> **86** Give customers choices in how they do business with you.

SHORTENING THE SUPPLY CHAIN

For organizations that operate through a supply chain, the Internet offers the opportunity to shorten the chain and get much closer to the customers. This increases flexibility, helps increase profits, and allows the company to research, develop, and introduce new products more quickly. Beware, however, of forgetting your existing supply chain. The Internet model is an additional chain, not a replacement. Find ways to use the Internet to support existing trade partners and help them get closer to your customers in order to provide a better service.

MANUFACTURER

Purchases made via traditional supply chain

WHOLESALER

Purchases made online through Internet reseller

INTERNET RESELLER

Purchases made online direct from manufacturer

RETAILER

CUSTOMERS

◄ LETTING THE CUSTOMER CHOOSE
Use the Internet to give customers the best possible service, whether the product is bought online or in offline stores.

IMPROVING CUSTOMER SERVICE

Because the Internet provides instant access to many competing suppliers, thereby ensuring that customers can always compare prices, it encourages ferocious price competition. In order to compete, organizations are increasingly focusing on customer service to differentiate themselves from competitors. Look for ways to engage with your customers, and design a website that provides quick and easy access to product information and after-sales help. Look at your organization from the outside in, and try to demolish all barriers to communication.

▼ **REACHING CUSTOMERS**
This case study shows the benefits of designing your Web site so that it gives your customers easy access to the information for which they are searching. It is important that it also provides good after-sales support service.

CASE STUDY
A leading electrical and electronic goods manufacturer decided to use its website to provide better customer service than that of its competitors, who focused on using the Web for sales material but gave few extra services.

After consulting with its real-world supply chain, the company decided to create a Web presence that would provide customers with the information they needed and help existing retailers by directing customers to them.

The resulting website helps customers find the product they need (and is even able to customize some products) and then gives them the choice of purchasing online or being directed to the nearest or most convenient retailer.

The extensive customer-support features include discussion groups, mailing lists, and live, text-based contact with support staff.

87	Monitor the ways in which your competitors deal with customers.

88	Encourage and facilitate customer contact online or with human staff.

UNDERSTANDING THE PITFALLS

Although many organizations talk about customer service, and claim to be committed to it, the perception of many customers is the opposite. Do not underestimate the power of the Internet audience to damage your reputation if you fail to perform. There is very little loyalty on the Web; customers can move to your competitor with the click of a mouse. Constantly monitor the way customers use your website to find ways to improve it. Make sure that the site is not a barrier to communication. Too many sites give no real-world contact details and seek to prevent contact with human staff, rather than encouraging communication in any way the customer chooses.

BUILDING THE SUPPLIER RELATIONSHIP

Close cooperation with each organization in your supply chain is essential if you are to minimize costs and maximize your flexibility. Take advantage of Internet technologies to share information and build closer relationships with suppliers.

 89 Post specifications on your intranet and let suppliers bid for contracts.

90 Give your staff an incentive to share information.

91 Seek users' input when building an intranet.

IMPROVING YOUR PURCHASING ABILITY

Fast communication between all members of a supply chain has become vital to minimize time-to-market, stock holdings, and just-in-time production. Electronic Data Interchange (EDI) was developed to facilitate fast transfer of repetitive business data. EDI used to be sent over expensive, private networks with many system incompatibility problems. Today, the Internet offers lower costs and more flexibility, enabling information to be easily shared with partners.

ASSESSING SUPPLIERS' READINESS FOR E-BUSINESS

It is important to identify which suppliers are ready and able to conduct business with you electronically. Ask your suppliers pertinent questions, focusing on their ability to share data using the Internet or a private intranet.

❝ *Do you have an intranet to enable easy sharing of data?* ❞

❝ *How much of your business with customers like us is conducted electronically?* ❞

❝ *Can we track our orders by accessing your extranet?* ❞

❝ *Can we access your stock database online and in real time to check stock levels?* ❞

USING AN INTRANET AND EXTRANET

An intranet is an internal website to which access is restricted to chosen audiences. Many companies use an intranet to share information within their organization. By using low-cost and flexible Internet technology, an intranet can also replace paper-based information. The value of an intranet can be extended by giving access to suppliers and, in some cases, important customers. This system is often referred to as an extranet. Create an extranet to share important information quickly with your partners and to allow them online, real-time access to selected data.

▼ INTERNAL WEBSITES
Building an intranet can be quick, easy, and cost-effective. You should delegate to individual departments some of the reponsibilities for creating and updating information.

Access your intranet on the office network, or via the Internet when traveling.

POINTS TO REMEMBER

- To benefit your customers, you and your suppliers should be able to share information quickly.

- Smaller organizations who have not used EDI before will need encouragement to explore the benefits of fast and accurate data-sharing via your extranet.

- Business-to-business transactions are expected to form the largest share of electronic commerce.

- Many large organizations are requiring companies to conduct business electronically before they can quote for contracts.

HELPING YOUR SUPPLY CHAIN

The development of EDI allowed large organizations to form electronic links with their most important suppliers and customers. The cost and complexity of EDI meant, however, that many smaller organizations could not take part in the information-sharing. Now, any size of organization can benefit from shared information by using Internet technologies. Aim to share as much information as possible with your business partners to ensure short production and delivery times, and to minimize costs or quality problems. Work with all partners in the supply chain to add value, reduce costs, and improve flexibility.

RESEARCHING ON THE WEB

The Internet provides rapid access to free or low-cost information that can give you commercial advantage if you learn how to use it better or faster than your competitors. Find out how to use search engines, and to conduct research effectively.

92 Remember, the Internet is a gold mine, but you have to do the mining.

93 Learn how the major search engines work.

94 Try searching Newsgroups as well as the Web.

USING SEARCH ENGINES

All search engines offer a simple search facility to help you locate information. Very often, however, a simple search returns too many results. Use the advanced search option to enter more key words, and to use powerful "Boolean-logic" searches that reduce the quantity and improve the quality of results. To do this, pick two or three leading search engines and study their search help files.

SPEEDING RESEARCH

The Internet is an enormous global resource of information on every subject imaginable, but it is also very unstructured. Finding the information you want, while avoiding a deluge of useless material, can be a challenge unless you learn how to search the Internet efficiently. To help solve this problem, Internet search engines create databases or catalogs of Web pages. Use these as your starting point. No one search engine is sufficient. Even the best cover less than half of Web content, so pick a few of the leading ones to use regularly.

DO'S AND DON'TS

✔ Do get to know how to use the top two or three leading search engines.

✔ Do explore the instructions for using advanced search features.

✔ Do think of several appropriate key words before starting your search.

✔ Do focus on finding information you need, and ignore the rest.

✘ Don't expect to get full coverage from just one or two search engines.

✘ Don't restrict yourself by using only the simple search function of a search engine.

✘ Don't search using very general words or phrases that will find too many results.

✘ Don't allow yourself to be sidetracked by irrelevant information.

GETTING CUSTOMER FEEDBACK

Customer feedback can be very valuable if it can be obtained quickly and cheaply, and then acted on efficiently. The unique communication power of the Internet provides an ideal means for conducting customer research and processing results. Build communication with your audience and encourage customer feedback using your website, email, mailing lists, and forums or discussion groups. Consider using online customer focus groups to test new product ideas, and to help refine your marketing strategies.

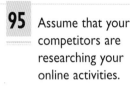

95 Assume that your competitors are researching your online activities.

▼ **KEEPING IN TOUCH WITH YOUR CUSTOMERS**
Customer focus is vital when operating on the Web. Aim to be the best in your industry at seeking customer feedback and acting on knowledge you receive. Try to reward each customer for their input.

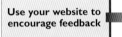

| Use your website to encourage feedback | Respond quickly to show you listen | Use feedback to improve services |

FINDING OUT ABOUT YOUR COMPETITORS

If your competitors have an Internet presence, you can use it to track their activities and even to predict their actions. Analyze their websites to see how they present themselves online, whether they sell products from their site, and how they handle customer relations. Use search engines to find pages on their site that may not have links from public areas but are accessible if you find their address. Look for ways they collect customer data and any password-protected areas for business customers or suppliers. Be aware, however, that many websites deposit "cookies" (small text files) in your browser to identify you and track your movements on the site. Do not accept these if you are viewing the site from your network, as your competitor may recognize your address and be able to monitor you researching their site.

POINTS TO REMEMBER

- The sophistication of your competitors' websites can indicate how committed they are to Internet commerce.
- Strange characters in an URL suggest you are being closely tracked around the site.
- Knowing which sites link to your competitors' is useful knowledge that will help you to compete online.

96 To improve your browsing privacy, set your browser to reject cookies.

MARKETING ON THE INTERNET

The Internet has become a vital business tool because it has the power to reach an enormous audience while giving you the ability to talk directly to individuals. Learning how to market your brand on the Internet is already essential for survival.

PUTTING YOUR BRAND ON THE WEB

Whether you have a real-world presence, or exist solely as an online organization, your brand is your most valuable asset. In the online world, where customers cannot see or touch your products, it is your brand values that create confidence and encourage customers to do business with you. The virtual world is so vast, though, that however well-known your brand is in the real world, it is easy to get lost in the commercial noise online. Fortunately, the Internet allows you to target your audiences closely and concentrate your efforts on niche markets. Work hard to identify the niche markets for your brand and use your online presence to contribute to your audience. Always aim to give added-value to online customers as no other method will build repeat business and loyalty.

97 Think of the Web as a very large number of small communities.

98 Remember that small competitors can be big online.

▼ TAPPING INTO NICHE MARKETS
A great strength of the Web is the ability it gives you to reach small interest groups and do business with them cost-effectively. Develop long-term relationships by giving added-value service.

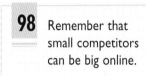

CASE STUDY
The butcher in a small Texas town understood that the Internet was an opportunity to increase his business.
He realized that he should target Web users interested in food, who would pay extra for high-quality, home-grown meat products.
Knowing that he needed to offer something very special to gain attention and draw repeat visits, he developed a website which offers mouth-watering recipes that change with the seasons. The site was created with a Texas theme, and stressed the qualities of local, speciality meats, with features on the local environment.
The website was designed to enable customers to order quickly online and pay by credit card through a secure server. Next-day delivery was guaranteed within the US..
Tapping the strengths of the Internet, the service created a valuable niche market.

Focuses on adding value for each visitor

Web address is simple and memorable

Respects your brand and creates a positive presence for it

Creates a two-way dialogue with customers

Has good information and easy navigation

Is fast to load to avoid frustrating visitors to the site

PROMOTING YOUR PRESENCE

Promote your Internet presence in the real world at least as much as you do online. Integrate on-line activities into all your offline promotions and seek to grab your audience's attention in both the real and online worlds. Even purely online brands, with no physical main street presence, must use extensive marketing and promotion in other media if they are to become known and trusted. Online, place "click-through" ads on sites that attract large numbers from your target audience. These send visitors direct to your site.

▲ CREATING AN EFFECTIVE WEBSITE

To do your brand justice, your website should have an effective address, be quick to load and simple to navigate, and must give every visitor good value.

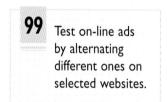

99 Test on-line ads by alternating different ones on selected websites.

POINTS TO REMEMBER

- Websites should not be designed like brochures if visitors are to be encouraged to return often.
- Ads can be used on other popular sites to attract visitors. Effectiveness should be tracked.
- New ways to use conventional direct marketing methods online should be actively sought.
- Always monitor your main competitors' online marketing and compare it with your own.

LAUNCHING INTO DIRECT MARKETING ONLINE

Direct marketing works extremely well online because the Internet facilitates one-to-one contact. Conventional loyalty and retention campaigns are effective and important to keep customers. Direct marketing on the Internet has the major advantage of allowing an organization to track results easily and get fast feedback when testing new marketing campaigns. To collect good-quality information you need visitors to part with personal details. Provide real incentives to encourage participants.

LAUNCHING E-COMMERCE

Setting up shop to sell on the Internet is a low-cost and quick process compared to opening premises in the real world. This means, however, that barriers to entry are low. In order to stay ahead of others, you must learn how to benefit from e-commerce.

 100 Watch others' e-commerce efforts closely to learn what works.

SETTING UP SHOP

Your website is your storefront on the Internet, and its design must reflect the fact that you have something to sell online. Early websites were little more than electronic brochures, but an e-commerce site requires careful attention to structure, design, and content issues if it is to be successful. When planning to open an e-commerce site, remember that you must offer convenience, savings, and added-value if you are to attract and keep online shoppers. Crucially, you must also be able to fulfill orders quickly. This requires an efficient "back-end" operation to cope with the level of orders.

Company appoints consultant to advise on e-commerce

Employee aware of potential of e-commerce puts proposal to manager

Manager fails to take up suggestion

101 Use the savings made from selling online to reduce your prices.

CULTURAL DIFFERENCES

English is the dominant language of the Internet, but it is important to remember that the audience is global. If you plan to sell online to an international audience, you should take the trouble to have versions of your site in all the major languages. Also ensure that you take account of national taxes and import duties when you sell across national frontiers.

TAKING PAYMENTS ONLINE

Taking online payments is simple to arrange. Many ISPs offer the use of "shopping cart" software and a secure server, and you can set up an online business account. For credit card payments, choose between real time or batch authorization. If you sell downloadable software or information online, real-time card-checking is important, but batch checking is cheaper.

Company appoints designer to create effective website

A year later, manager reports a sharp rise in online profits and discusses expansion of the business

A year later, manager realizes his business is not keeping up with competitors

POINTS TO REMEMBER

- An e-commerce site must be designed to be quick and simple for customers to use.
- An online business account can usually be set up quickly.
- Customer use of your website should be monitored carefully.
- Your site should be developed in response to customer feedback, which you must actively seek.

TARGETING YOUR AUDIENCE

Ensure your website is designed to be fast and easy for visitors to use. Do not use large graphics that result in slow downloads, or your customers will go elsewhere. If you are selling a product from the site, make the fact clear to visitors, and include prominent pointers to your sales catalog on each page. Provide good information on products, and make sure that the site is designed to ask for, and close, the sale.

ASSESSING YOUR IT SKILLS

Remember that the skills required for managing IT take time and effort to develop, but it is essential to learn them. Evaluate your performance by responding to the following statements, marking the option closest to your experience. Be as honest as you can: if your answer is "never," circle option 1; if it is "always," circle option 4, and so on. Add your scores together, and refer to the Analysis to see how you scored. Use your answers to identify which skills or attitudes need development or improvement.

OPTIONS
1 Never
2 Occasionally
3 Frequently
4 Always

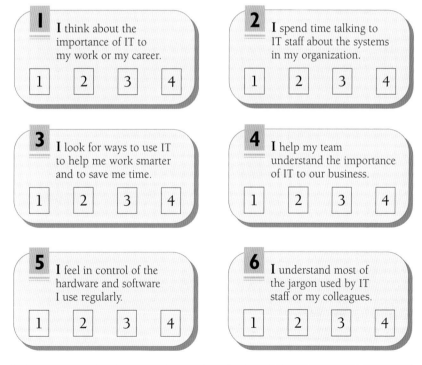

1 I think about the importance of IT to my work or my career.

1 2 3 4

2 I spend time talking to IT staff about the systems in my organization.

1 2 3 4

3 I look for ways to use IT to help me work smarter and to save me time.

1 2 3 4

4 I help my team understand the importance of IT to our business.

1 2 3 4

5 I feel in control of the hardware and software I use regularly.

1 2 3 4

6 I understand most of the jargon used by IT staff or my colleagues.

1 2 3 4

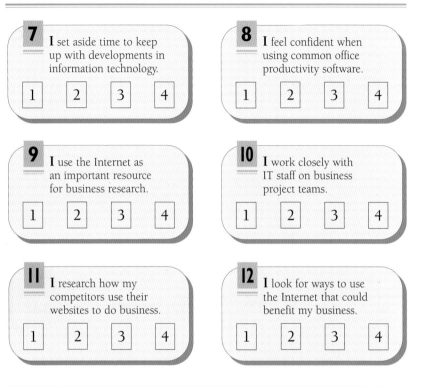

7 I set aside time to keep up with developments in information technology.

1   2   3   4

8 I feel confident when using common office productivity software.

1   2   3   4

9 I use the Internet as an important resource for business research.

1   2   3   4

10 I work closely with IT staff on business project teams.

1   2   3   4

11 I research how my competitors use their websites to do business.

1   2   3   4

12 I look for ways to use the Internet that could benefit my business.

1   2   3   4

ANALYSIS

Now you have completed the self-assessment, add up the total score and check your performance by referring to the corresponding evaluation below. Whatever level of success you achieved in managing IT, remember that technology moves on rapidly, and make an effort to keep in touch with developments. Identify your weakest areas, and refer to the relevant sections in this book for guidance.

12–24: You need to work on developing your skills if you are to be able to use IT to benefit you and your organization.
25–36: You have a sound grasp of many IT issues: review your weaker areas to improve your expertise.
37–48: Your understanding of IT and its importance to your business is good: focus on keeping up to date.

INDEX

ACKNOWLEDGMENTS

AUTHOR'S ACKNOWLEDGMENTS

Although the author has the privilege, and the responsibility, of his or her name on the cover, a book is invariably the product of a hard-working team. This book is no exception, and thanks are due to the editors and designers at both Cactus and Dorling Kindersley for their enthusiasm and professionalism. I also wish to thank all those who, over the last twenty years or so, have thaught me about IT, and most especially the brave ones who gave me the freedom to experiment with new ideas.

PUBLISHER'S ACKNOWLEDGMENTS

Dorling Kindersley would like to thank the following for their help and participation:

Editorial Jane Simmonds; **Design** Sharon Moore; **DTP assistance** Jason Little; **Indexer** Hilary Bird; **Proofreader** John Sturges; **Photography** Steve Gorton, Richard Parsons; **Photographer's assistant** Andrew Komorowski.

Models Roger André, Philip Argent, Clare Borg, Angela Cameron, Anne Chapman, Kuo Kang Chen, Felicity Crowe, Patrick Dobbs, Carole Evans, Vosjava Fahkro, John Gillard, Richard Hill, Cornell John, Zahid Malik, Frankie Mayers, Sotiris Melioumis, Karen Murray, Chantal Newall, Kiran Shah, Suki Tan, Peter Taylor, Ann Winterborn, Gilbert Wu; **Make-up** Nicky Clarke.

Special thanks to the following for their help throughout the series:

Pam Bennett and the staff at Jones Bootmakers, Covent Garden, for the loan of footwear; Alan Pfaff and the staff at Moss Bros, Covent Garden, for the loan of the men's suits; David Bailey for his help and time; Graham Preston and the staff at Staverton for their time and space.

Suppliers Apple Computer UK Ltd., Cadogan and James, Gieves and Hawkes, Marc Holman, Mucci Bags, Positive (Computing), Viper Microsystems.

Picture researcher Andy Sansom; **Picture librarian** Melanie Simmonds

PICTURE CREDITS

The publisher would like to thank the following for their kind permission to reproduce their photographs:

Key: *b*=bottom; *c*=centre; *l*=left; *r*=right; *t*=top;
©1995-2000 Agfa-Gevaert Group: 20; ©2000 Apple Computer Inc: 43tr;
BT Archives/Pictures: 23tc; Compaq Computer Corp: 23c; ©2000 Iomega Corporation: 21tr;
Powerstock Photolibrary/Zefa:40, 48; **Science Photo Library:** George Bernard 17b;
Rex Interstock: Richard Fitzgerald (front jacket); **Tony Stone Images:** Dan Bosler 56;
Paul Kenward 34; Robert Mort 8; **Telegraph Colour Library:** Jim Cummings 4.

AUTHOR'S BIOGRAPHY

Steve Sleight is an author and independent consultant with considerable experience in IT. As a director of a European sponsorship consultancy, he was responsible for the strategic use of IT, setting up connected IT networks, and managing the use of IT resources. Most recently, he managed four major projects for a leading car distributor. With a background in writing, broadcasting, and communications, Steve Sleight is now concentrating on producing digital, multimedia content that can be presented and delivered in traditional or new media forms. He writes on business subjects as well as on his real, all-consuming passion, sailing. He is the author of the DK *Complete Sailing Manual*.